Passionate About Picnics

A Picnic for every Season in and around New Castle County, Delaware

Mary W. Davis

Happy Picnicking!
Mary W Davis

For information or permission to use excerpts, please contact: Mary Davis at mfwdavis@gmail.com

Softbound Edition: ISBN: 978-1-4951-5743-1

Printed in the United States of America by United Book Press, Baltimore, MD

Mary Wolcott Davis is a native Delawarean whose family has deep roots in all three counties. She enjoys explo... corner of the state with friends and family. Mary is a mental health therapist in private practice in Wilmington, Delaware.

Inspired by the memorable picnics she experienced with her friends and family, Mary wrote this book to share the "seasonal serendipity," in other words, grab the moment and go!

My happy band of Picnickers!
Bob, Liza, Mary, Wolcott and Wil.

This book is dedicated to, and I am devoted to, my faithful picnic companions – Bob, Wil, Wolcott and Liza.
We've spent many happy, tranquil hours together, which will never be forgotten by any of us. And special acknowledgement to our occasional picnic companions, Lisa, Kate, Nick, Joe and Para, Dick and Barbara, Merritt, Dan and Cindy, and Geoff and Alice, who have shared with us the pleasures of a perfect picnic. As it turns out, it takes a village to write a book about picnics! Utmost thanks to my sister, Lisa, for her suggestions and who never stopped believing that I would write this!

And thank you, especially, to my husband, Bob, who not only joined me on every picnic, tried every recipe with me, but lived patiently with piles of picnic baskets, books, papers in every closet and corner of our house. He has supported me in every way.

And there are lots of you, too, that have heard about this book for quite some time and encouraged me! Can't thank you enough!

- Table of Contents -

PENNSYLVANIA

NEW JERSEY

Stateline Woods
Preserve

Marshall House
Preserve

Woodlawn
Tract

52

Winterthur

Brandywine
Creek State Park

Valley Garden
Park

Alapocas Run
State Park

Caufield House

41

Breck's Mill

95

Bellevue State
Park

141

London Tract
Meeting House

Russell W. Peterson
Wildlife Refuge

River

White Clay Creek
Preserve

72

295

Battery Park

Riverview
Park

Delaware

Hancock House
at Hancock's Bridge

DELAWARE

Fort Dupont

Susquehanna
State Park, MD

Historic
Odessa

Alapocas Run State Park -
West Park Drive, Wilmington, DE 19803

Battery Park - New Castle, DE 19720

Bellevue State Park -
800 Carr Road, Wilmington, DE 19809

Brandywine Creek State Park -
47 Adams Dam Road, Wilmington, Delaware 19807

Breck's Mill - Stone Block Row, Greenville, DE 19807

Caufield House -
1016 Philadelphia Pike, Wilmington, DE 19809

Fort DuPont - Delaware City, DE 19706

Hancock House at Hancock's Bridge -
Lower Alloway Creek, New Jersey 08038

Historic Odessa - 109 Main Street, Odessa, DE 19730

London Tract Meeting House -
London Tract Road, Landenberg, PA 19350

Marshall House -
932 Creek Road, Kennett Square, PA 19348

Russell W. Peterson Wildlife Refuge -
1400 Delmarva Lane, Wilmington, DE 19801

Stateline Wood Preserve -
814 Merry Bell Lane, Kennett Square, PA 19348

Susquehanna State Park -
3700-3799 Rock Run Road, Havre de Grace, MD 21078

Valley Garden Park - Greenville, DE 19807

White Clay Creek, Newark, Delaware

White Clay Creek Preserve -
London Tract Road, Landenberg, PA 19350

Winterthur Museum -
5105 Kennett Pike, Wilmington, DE 19735

Woodlawn Tract - First State National Historical Park
Beaver Dam Road and Creek Road, Wilmington, DE 19807

Introduction

Think of it! The school year is over. Spring activities have come and gone and summer is before you beckoning with its warmth, sultry air, lazy days and long evenings. The rivers and ocean are sparkling, the sky is blue with big puffy clouds and the birds swoop and sing from daybreak until soft, blue twilight.

For me, that means picnic season. Picnics are good for the soul and the spirit. They can be relaxing or adventuresome.

They can be magical, unrepeatable moments or they can be duds. It doesn't matter. However your picnic turns out, you will have a million memories.

Picnics are for everyone.-rich, poor, singles, lovers, old married couples, families or friends. There is nothing more satisfying than packing up the picnic basket, readying the cooler and setting off to a beautiful location and enjoying what the season and countryside have to offer.

This book will introduce you to a world of experiences with the people you love. Bugs, forgotten corkscrews, overturned drinks in the main dish, soggy sandwiches are incidentals that can happen along the way with any picnic but the relationships enjoyed and the bright spots they will create for you are worth every second.

I've been on a lot of picnics with my trusty band and we are experts. This book is a tribute to them and an offering to you that you may renew your spirits.

- Picnic Ware and Fare -

A complete list of things you will need for picnicking

Picnic Basket

We love our picnic baskets. We've got a little one for a twosome, a traditional one that was my mother's, and even an Adirondack picnic backpack! But our very favorite one is the one we rescued from the pile of discards our neighbors were ready to send to the local flea market. It has since been our faithful companion.

Picnic Blanket

We don't really consider a picnic a picnic unless we are sitting on a blanket– one per person and two for the food. And we don't really use blankets. We use our wonderful collection of table cloths-some are vintage from our mothers summer dinner tables, some we've found along the way in antique shops and some have been gifts from our fellow picnickers.

Cooler

A cooler is essential. Two small coolers are easier to handle than one large one. And a rolling cooler is a plus.

Large Canvas Bag

An extra bag is always necessary for the extras.

Back Pack

A must have for picnics where you want to go simple or have to hike in a ways.

Plates

If they are paper– be sure they're the sturdy type. We do use washable, sturdy plastic ones too. Easy to pop into a bag at the end and stick in the dishwasher when you get home.

Flatware

We like to use real flatware. It's so much nicer. There's nothing less fun than trying to eat your picnic fare with a tiny little plastic fork. But you can buy silver look alike plastic silverware in the grocery store– a nice touch!

Napkins

We usually use paper but for our fancy picnics we bring our multi colored cloth ones.

Paper towels

Stick a roll in the canvas bag– comes in handy!

Cups and Bowls

We always use paper for cups-any size works. And you can buy paper or plastic bowls or cups for soup.

Plastic Containers

One of the best things about picnics is that you can throw everything away after the picnic– no fuss, no muss! I save all my plastic containers during the year to use for picnicking– even little spice jars are useful for dips etc. Of course, being environmentally minded, I take them home, rinse them out and chuck them into the recycling bin. But even that doesn't feel like work. The cupboard where I keep all of the containers is quite dangerous-no one in the family dares to open the door!

Continued

Continued

Bottles of water	Always useful for washing hands and cleaning up any mishaps
Trash Bags	Bring one for trash, one for dishes and flatware and one for recyclables
Can of Mixed Nuts	Always have these in your basket - they can get you through the most desperate of failed picnic food moments!
Grill	Buy a supply of disposable grills – easy to douse with water and chuck when you are ready to head for home

Small sharp knife

Tree, bird and flower identification books

Deck of Playing Cards

Bug Spray	a DEET based bug spray will keep everyone complaint and bite free

Sun screen, A radio

A camera to record your memories

This is the complete list– of course, you may want to stream line it.

A few things to remember:

Be sure to clean up EVERYTHING from your picnic. Obviously you won't leave your trash but don't leave any of your food. The wildlife is not accustomed to it and it confuses their natural instincts to search for food.

Think about food safety. Check foodsafety@ncsu.edu but don't let it scare you into staying home!

Follow all rules and regs of any park or public space. Some are more relaxed than others.

We do love our picnic ware.

Baskets both big and small, table cloths, some of which adorned our mothers' summer dinner tables, the old minnow bucket that serves as a cooler, devilled egg carriers, perfect plastic plates, backpacks, the canvas bag with the aqua trim that just looks like summer and so on.

The more picnics you take the more you will come to love the equipment that you have gathered over time. And that is now taking up half the garage!

(just kidding) (but not really!)

A few thoughts about what to eat.

We have found that less is more. Simple is better. From time to time a lavish picnic can be fun but if you really want to go on more than one picnic in a decade…....keep it simple! Preparing your picnic can be done the day before and saved in the refrigerator. When you are ready to go all you have to do is pack it up-which is half the fun! And although you have done some cooking and preparing, by the time you get to your picnic, it's as if you have the night off. And for those days when you really don't feel like cooking, you can go to a local grocery store. Pick-up some good bread, interesting items from the deli, good mustard, fresh fruit and some good cookies and you'll be on your way.

The Basic Essentials Plus

Start with a cold soup-this really sets the tone, curbs the ravenous appetites and brings on a sense of relaxation. Nothing like leaning against a rock in the woods or lying near the flowing Brandywine, sipping on an elegant cold soup (which you would never have at home) to remind you that the worries of the day have slipped away on the evening breeze. Cold soups are easy and very seasonal with the local vegetables to be found. Cold cucumber, fresh tomato with basil, red peppers, cream of zucchini soup- summer's bounty!

A baguette and cheese- both are a necessity. Makes everyone feels elegant and like a true picnicker! Serve it with the cold soup. We especially love triple crème brie-one never tires of its exquisite taste and creamy texture.

Mixed nuts– a handy staple that can save the day!

Main course– There are lots of ways to go with the main course. Sturdy finger foods are good as are pasta salads, exotic couscous or quinoa salads loaded with fresh vegetables , and the all time number one favorite– chicken salad. And don't forget the devilled eggs! Remember, keep it simple! Only cook a couple of things– purchased items are (almost) as good!

Dessert– a bite of sweet is all you need for the finishing touch as the sun is setting. A bit of fancy chocolate and some fresh fruit, a transportable fruity cobbler that can be served at room temperature is all your fellow picnic feasters will want.

With every picnic in this book I've shared our menus and some of the recipes. The ones I've shared are tried and true. No need to let you in on the flops!

- Seasonal Picnics -

- Early Spring Picnics -

Brandywine Creek State Park
Rockford Falls

There is nothing lovelier than an early Spring picnic. The greens of the leaves are so vivid, the pinks are so pink. All is new, fresh and an amazing surprise each year. Somehow we forget what it's like during the long winter. One of the most beautiful picnics I have had was up a rocky run along the Brandywine River. You'll want to pack a light back pack as you'll be making your way along some rocks. It's perfectly safe. But do take care. The water bubbling through the rocks, the gifts of nature that might visit you, all make for a revitalizing moment. This a contemplative type of picnic so venture out alone or with just one other person.

I like to park in the little parking lot at Rockland Falls (Rockland Road, Rockland DE)– there is a parking fee.

The pair of red buds mark the main trail. Walk about 15 minutes. The single red bud will tell you where the Rocky Run is. Scramble up the run a ways– find a flattish rock to sit on and enjoy the friends that might join you!

- Suggested Menu -

Mixed nuts

Brie or your favorite spreadable cheese
with Baguette

Cold Zucchini Soup (see recipes)

Thinly sliced beef or pork tenderloin
(Make sandwiches with
the brie and baguette)

Your favorite pasta salad

An apple

Cookies

It's Bluebell Season!

Spring has such ephemeral pleasures. Catch them while you can! Don't waste a minute to set out in pursuit of their miraculous return year after year. In summer you can count on the solid green and shade of summer and let the days pass by one by one and wait until next week to plan your picnic. But Spring taunts you with the day wasted indoors as she beckons from beyond. Grab on to her while you can. Next week may be too late– she'll be gone.

Bluebells and the Susquehanna

We heard about this special place and set off on a glorious Saturday in early Spring. The drive alone was a pleasure but what awaited us was even more! We didn't expect to discover the Red Rock Historic Area that is from a world long gone of a grist mill and its owner's mansion set on a hill near by. An old toll house tells of the busy life along the beautiful Susquehanna.

Driving Directions
95 South to Exit 93-Route 222 toward Perryville and Port Deposit. Take 222 N to toward Port Deposit. At the T (about 2 miles) turn left onto 276-S toward Port Deposit. In about 2 miles turn right onto Main Street of Port Deposit. Follow along about 5 miles– lovely drive with the woods filled with native Dogwood and Redbuds. Go to Route 1 and cross over the Conowingo Dam . Very soon you will take a left onto Shuresville Road which will take you through an adorable little town. Continue on through some lovely horse country.

Park at the bottom of the hill– there is lots of history to see and read about but it is the abundance of beautiful flowers of early spring that will make your day. Bluebells– blue, pink and white ones, Dutchmen's Britches, Spring Beauties, Phlox, Trillium, Fiddlehead Ferns ready to pop, Violets– purple and white, Jacks in the Pulpit, Cut Leaf Tooth Wart and the famous Paw-Paw. If you have a cool day consider picnicking in Deer Creek Picnic Park. It is a lovely green expanse. If you feel like carrying your lunch in a backpack, walk back along the road and cross over the mill stream. Walk 3 minutes past the beehive shaped oven and look for a lovely spot along the water.

Susquehanna State Park
3700-3799 Rock Run Road Havre de Grace MD, 21078

- Suggested Menu -

Cucumber Dill Soup (see recipes)

Bob's Toast Points (see recipes)

Spreadable cheese

Slices of roast chicken

Cold Asparagus with
cocktail sauce for dipping

Fruit and Chocolate

- Summer Picnics -

Russell W. Peterson Wildlife Refuge

1400 Delmarva Lane, Wilmington, DE 19801

Down by the Waterfront– Go past the Chase Center and keep driving. This refuge is named for Russell Peterson, former governor of Delaware and internationally recognized conservationist who worked to preserve Delaware's natural spaces. Desperate to begin our picnic season we decided on this spot as an easy destination. It was early in the season and we didn't need shade– just wanted to bask in the sun like the turtles here!

This unique spot is perfect for an early spring or summer picnic. Enjoy the sun on your backs as you watch the water fowl, fish and turtles from the dock. We kept our picnic simple as a pre-season opener.

- Suggested Menu -

Brie and Baguette

Cream of Curry Soup (see recipes)

Pork Loin with Mouffelata spread (see recipes)

Crunchy fresh vegetables

Fruit

Cookies and chocolate bars

- Lazy, Hazy Picnic -

Woodlawn Tract

First State National Park, Beaver Dam Road and Creek Road

- Suggested Menu -

Baguette and Brie
(or any yummy cheese)

Cold Avocado and Cucumber Soup
(see Recipe)

Barbecued Chicken, however you like it

Quinoa Salad (see recipes)

Devilled eggs

Fresh Fruit

Sugar Cookies

One of our favorite spots– in fact, the picnic we had here may have been where it all began. Along the banks of the Brandywine, watching the swallows swoop down to get their evening meal of insects and seeing the dragon flies buzz by made for a perfect picnic evening. The gold of the sunset behind the trees was inspiring. Occasionally, the shouts of children interrupted the tranquility or an occasional motorcycle came around the corner strutting its stuff but they were all the happy sounds of summer.

There are two ways to enjoy a picnic at this spot. One is to sit on the wide grassy bank near the parking lot. You can pack a basket and cooler and enjoy a more sumptuous picnic. The other is to park along the side of the road after you have passed the parking lot and the curve in the road (if you are coming from the other direction you can turn around in the parking lot). Walk down the road and enter the park by going to the left. Take the unpaved trail and find a spot where you can go down by the water. Just pack a light picnic in your backpack. This is quite a popular place on the weekends in the summer so either go early or go late or choose a weekday evening!

Bang Up 4th of July!

What a beautiful place Winterthur is to picnic! If you aren't a member you are missing out. As a member, you are permitted to explore the estate and borrow the views and enjoy the shady spots. I love picnicking at Winterthur—one is transported to another world far away from traffic and people but 5 minutes from civilization. We had a lovely Fourth of July celebration on Sycamore Hill. Explore and discover other secret and solitary spots where you can take in seemingly endless summer evenings. You can dine on Sycamore Hill, picnic next to Clenny Run and even take the children to picnic next to Enchanted Woods. Consider packing a light picnic in a backpack and wile away the evening on one of the many surrounding hills. Google Winterthur picnic for answers to frequently asked questions. Sad as it is, when the fireflies come out it is time to head home!

Winterthur Museum, Garden and Library
5105 Kennett Pike, Wilmington, DE 19735

- Suggested Menu -
An all American Picnic!

Mixed Nuts

Grilled Cheese Sandwiches

served at room temperature
(instead of Brie and a Baguette!)

Roasted Tomato Soup
(see recipes)

Fried Chicken

Potato Salad

Cole slaw

Fresh crunchy vegetables and dip

Blueberry Tarts (See recipes)

*"I sincerely hope that....visitors may enjoy as I have,
not only the flowers ,trees and shrubs,
but also the sunlit meadows, shady garden paths,
and the peace and great calm of a country place
which has been loved and cared for by three generations"*

Henry Francis duPont

Stateline Woods Preserve

The Land Conservancy for Southern Chester County
814 Merry Bell Lane, Kennett Square, PA 19348 (off of Old Kennett Pike)

This beautiful preserve is so densely packed with trees that on a summer evening you will be 15 degrees cooler. The quiet and majesty of the trees is Mother Nature's Cathedral. Rocks have been strewn by her to be your back rest. When you arrive, take the path that leads to the right to reach the "nave" of Mother Nature's Cathedral. Somehow we always manage to choose the hottest nights for our picnics! Everyone grumbles about going but once there, the beauty and stillness and coolness of the place takes over. Hearing the birds settle into their nests for the evening and relaxing against the rocks take us to another dimension.

You'll have to walk a little to get to the center of the "cathedral" so carry your picnic in a couple of backpacks.

- Suggested Menu -

Brie and Baguette
Smoked salmon and
Bob's Toast Points (see recipes)
Sliced Summer tomatoes
Antipasto (see recipes)
29Cookies and Fruit

Valley Garden Park

Greenville, DE 19807, (off Campbell Road at the Intersection of Route 52 N)

Don't ask me why this bountiful, beautiful park is practically empty every time we go there! This is a must when the evenings are longest because you will want to linger here. But they lock the gates at dusk and they aren't joking! The park overseer bellows out a warnings that can be heard country-wide! Truly this is a summer secret. Except for the random couple out walking, we were alone. This City of Wilmington park was once the estate of Ellen duPont Wheelwright. To get to a good spot you will walk by the remains of the outside theater with the trees over hanging and the occasional boxwood of the long gone formal gardens. There is lots of room to spread out your tablecloths, lie on your backs and wallow in the soft light of summer.

Be sure to picnic under the state champion Poplar tree!

- Suggested Menu -

Brie and Baguette

Bob's Pierogi (see recipes)

Salade Niçoise (see recipes)

Fancy Chocolate Bars and Fresh Fruit

- Big Tree Picnics -

In the summer, the shade of a tree calls to me. How many accidents have I almost caused admiring a tree as I drive by? I search for a patch of shade of a tree in which to park my car in the busiest of parking lots. Tall trees, shade, the rustling of the leaves soothe even the most troubled soul in the summer. The shade of a tree makes even the most humid day seem bearable. And think about it - isn't the day or evening made for idling under nature's parasol? Spread out your picnic blankets, bring your favorite basket , some good things to eat and you will spend the loveliest and least expensive summer day .This fun couple, Kurt and Rachel, had the right idea and were spending the day with Grady enjoying life.

Drive past the main parking area
and park near the tennis courts.
The magnificent trees are in front of the mansion.
Check at the park office for a tree guide.

Bellevue State Park
800 Carr Road, Wilmington, DE 19809

- Suggested Menu -

This is a great place to bring your favorite picnic things and to have an elegant luncheon next to the mansion.

In Kurt and Rachel's Basket were:

Chicken Salad Sandwiches

Pasta Salad

Sliced avocado tomato and cantaloupe

You might consider:

Mixed Nuts

Brie and Baguette

Cold Zucchini Soup (See Recipes)

Shute House Tomato Tart (see recipes)

Green Salad or crunchy vegetables and dip

Fruit Salad

Cookies

...and of course, treats for Grady!

Caufield House

1016 Philadelphia Pike, Wilmington DE 19809

Caulfield House is a lovely house with beautiful grounds that is part of Bellevue State Park. We picnicked here one evening on the front lawn that faces Philadelphia Pike and had the place to ourselves except for the gentle hum of the insects and the swooping of the evening birds in pursuit of their dinner. On a breezy summer day we picnicked in the gazebo on the back lawn overlooking the Delaware River and enjoyed the shadows and play of the light on the foliage. Caulfield House has some interesting old out buildings and a mini walk across Caulfield Connector. It's also fun to start in Rockwood Park or Bellevue State Park and make your way to the Gazebo.

- Suggested Menu -

Hot Summer Evening

Brie and Baguette

Barbecued Chicken

Watermelon, Barley, and

Black eyed Pea Salad (see recipes)

Blodg's Blueberry Dessert (see recipes)

Mixed nuts

Breezy Summer Day

Assorted Sandwiches (see recipes)

Potato chips

Fresh Fruit

Brownies

Brecks' Mill
Stone Block Row, Greenville DE 19807

Ready made picnicking along the Brandywine!

Not only does this wonderful old mill have a ready made stone bench built into the wall but there are lovely falls where you can (carefully) sit and put your feet in to cool off on a hot summer's evening. Don't worry if you drop a little of your dinner in the river—a happy fish will find it! On a very hot summer evening we came here to hear the rush of the water and just let that sound cool us off. It was quiet, no traffic and even the deer across the way came out to enjoy the evening.

- Suggested Menu -

John's Ceviche (see recipes)

Guacamole and chips

Sliced Tomatoes or Fruit Salad with
melon and watermelon

Picnic Pots de Crème (see recipes)

Historic Odessa

109 Main Street, Odessa, DE 9730

Growing up in New Castle and going to Rehoboth Beach we always took Route 9. This road has so many memories for everyone in my family. It is part of old Delaware that still exists. Our mood always brightens as we drive along through Delaware City, Port Penn, Augustine Beach, stop at the look out tower at Mallard Lodge, and continue on through Woodland Beach, Leipsic and Little Creek. One could spend a day along this road with the cooler and picnic basket on the back seat.

But a perfect picnicking spot is Historic Odessa. The Wilson-Warner House and the Corbit-Sharp House share a spacious lawn with lovely trees that is perfect for an evening picnic. Or you can go through the gates of the Corbit-Sharp House and find a delightful spot. Do spend some time walking about the town. It is a perfect mix of country and city.

The best way to get to this picnic is to start in New Castle and take Route 9 from there. Follow signs for Route 9. At the intersection of Routes 9 and 299-turn right and head into Odessa. Your picnic spot is across the street from the old bank building and Cantwell's Tavern.

- Suggested Menu -

Brie and Baguette

Chicken and Veggies on skewers
(see recipes)

Tortellini Salad

Texas Fudge
(a savory not a sweet– see recipes)

Fresh Fruit

Frozen Snickers Bars

London Tract Meeting House

London Tract Road, Landenberg, PA 19350
White Clay Creek Preserve - Home of the Ticking Tomb Stone!

Legend has it that when Charles Mason and Jeremiah Dixon were mapping the route for the Mason-Dixon line they encountered a young boy who stole and swallowed Mason's watch! And that watch is still ticking today! People claim that on a still evening you can hear it ticking away in his grave. As a boy, my husband, who grew up in Chester County, spent a scary Boy Scout all night initiation ritual in this very spot and still has not recovered!

This is just a short way into Pennsylvania and it is a beautiful spot for picnicking and walking. We are particularly fond of Landenberg and the London Tract churchyard makes a perfect setting for an evening of relaxation. We found a spot under one of the huge Paulownia trees. We headed out here on the hottest night of the summer. Not a car on the road because everyone was inside, afraid of the summer heat. The temperature was 15 degrees cooler and we enjoyed our cool, summer solitude. After your picnic, walk along the White Clay Creek. This is a great place to go with children. You can also walk along the path in the park and find a flat rock in the Creek for your picnic.

- Suggested Menu -

This is a place to have an elegant picnic. It's not too far to carry a fancy picnic basket and have a more elaborate meal. Here we used our colorful plastic plates and real silverware.

Cold Curry of Eggplant Soup (see recipes)

Chicken Salad with grapes and almonds

with

Ann's Blueberry Muffins (see recipe)

Sliced Cantaloupe

Baguette and Brie

Mixed nuts

Fancy chocolates for dessert

Marshall House Preserve

932 Creek Road (Route 82), Kennett Square, PA 19348

I don't mind the heat and humidity of a summer's day, especially when I know that being in the woods will provide me with tranquility and coolness. It was on such a summer's day that I discovered the Marshall Mill House Preserve. I was at loose ends that day and wanted to feel the embrace of the quiet, green woods.

This is a great spot for one of those days when you feel like being on your own. Or two people is good, too! This is one of the preserves of The Land Conservancy for Southern Chester County. Its charms include a bench at Robinson's Ridge just for you, as well as the beautiful, tall trees.

- Suggested Menu -

This is a back pack type of picnic so you will want to go minimal.

Skip the soup and go right to a sandwich.

Give your sandwich some flair
but be sure it's hearty –
one is always hungrier in the woods
(see recipes)

White grapes

Trail Mix

Cookies

Picnic floatng on the Brandywine!

My son and I set off on this adventure, not expecting the pleasures we encountered.

This has its complications but is beyond worth it! We found it a perfect way to spend a summer's day. For this picnic you'll need two cars and kayaks or big tubes for floating down the river. We have two inflatable, portable kayaks (good investment). Begin your day by dropping one car at The Woodlawn Estate/National Historic Landmark parking lot. After dropping one car off head out of the parking lot to the Brandywine River Museum on Route 1 in Chadd's Ford. You can launch from there. Sometimes they charge a small fee to park there. It's probably best to do this on a weekday in the summer as the river is popular and crowded on the weekends.

There are local companies who will provide kayaks, canoes or tubes as well as transportation. You'll have to supply the picnic!

Count on four hours of floating along the Brandywine.

- Suggested Menu -

Whatever you pack make sure it is light
enough not to weigh down your kayak.
I made a simple lunch from things I found in
the cupboard. I have some insulated bags
that I use with a blue freezer insert (a dime
a dozen at the supermarket) to keep things
cool.

Doctored up Campbell's tomato soup

Tuna fish salad sandwiches

Egg salad sandwiches
(put the egg salad and tuna fish salad
in baggies and put on top of the
freezer inserts and
assemble the sandwich on site).

Individual bags of potato chips

Pistachios in the shell

Fresh Fruit

White Clay Creek
Newark, Delaware

Breakfast in a Creek!

Summer is never better than in the morning. Participating in a 5K Run/Walk along the White Clay Creek on a Saturday, I spied a perfect spot for a breakfast picnic. It's not necessarily the easiest access but anyone who has a pair of shoes to wear in the water and doesn't mind getting a little wet will love it. And, of course, the kids will be clamoring to do this every day and it will be their favorite activity of the whole summer! You may have to carry a few things but the pain of that will be gone as soon as you've settled yourselves in this lovely spot! Be sure to take a couple of camping chairs– it will make life a little more comfy.

Driving Directions: 95 S to Newark/896 N. Drive all the way to Main Street and make a left onto Main Street. Take the first right onto North College Avenue. Keep driving and this will turn into a lovely, tree-lined narrow road. We parked along the side of the road in the first place where there was a spot to pull over and made our way down to the water. As this picnic spot is really for the most adventuresome of picnickers, a very nice alternative is Rittenhouse Park in Newark. There are lots of rocks or a little beach where the breakfasting will be lovely.

- Suggested Menu -

Coffee

Liza's Yogurt Smoothies (see recipes)

Blueberry Pancakes
(don't forget the syrup and butter)

Bisquick makes individual
containers of pancake mix
and all you do is add the water - simple!

Bacon
(pre cook until almost finished
before setting out)

Eggs– sunny side up

Fresh fruit

And yes,
we even lugged my mother's old iron griddle!

White Clay Creek Preserve

London Tract Road, Landenberg, PA 19350

Breakfast by a Creek

Breakfast picnics really can be the most fun of any. We set off early to take advantage of the stillness of the day and the early morning light.

Park in the parking lot #1 and enter the trail. There are numerous spots where you can picnic. What's lovely about having breakfast in or by a creek is that the expanse of the clear sky is above. The morning is cool and looking up at the corridor of sky created by the trees on the banks of the creek is, I guess, a fish's eye view. The only trouble with this picnic is that you won't want to go home!

- Suggested Menu -

Fresh fruit

Cinnamon Swirl French Toast

Eggs - Easy over

Bacon

Ann's Blueberry Muffins (see recipes)

Hot coffee

- Autumn Picnics -

Alapocas Run State Park

West Park Drive, Wilmington, Delaware 19803

A Child's Tea Party!

In winter we long for spring, In spring we long for summer and in summer we long for the cool, crisp days of Autumn. Days when we can really luxuriate in the sun, marvel at the yellow beech trees, the vibrant maples, and the unmistakable smell of autumn in the air.

Looking for something to do to entertain the siblings between dentist appointments and soccer games? Or just for a fun summer early morning adventure or late afternoon tea make your way to Alapocas Run State Park. There are two sides to the park, one along the Brandywine and the other heading to Blue Ball Barn. Along the way to Blue Ball Barn is a magical stopping off place– just right to set up tea party for the fairies!

Driving directions: Make your way to Alapocas by 141N or Augustine Cut-off. Park on the street on Edgewood Road. You will have to back track a little to enter the park– back track and then cross Alapocas Drive at the cross walk. Its not a good idea to walk along the road as the cars whiz by.

After crossing the road head up the trail for about 15 minutes (I know it sounds long with little ones but it's doable). On the right—after the second bridge – you will see an outcropping of rocks. And that's where the magic happens!

Relax and enjoy a respite from your busy life while the children have tea in this secret spot.

- Suggested Menu -

Bread and Jelly Sandwiches
cut from cookie cutters

Chocolate Shortbread Scones

Fresh fruit Kabobs

Brandywine Creek State Park

47 Adams Dam Road, Wilmington, DE 19807

Along the Brandywine

It really is unbelievable that we live right near the Brandywine. Every time I am near it I marvel at this wonder that we seem to take for granted. Any hour of any season that I come here I feel restored.

Almost anywhere along the Brandywine is a reminder about how fortunate we are to have such beauty right in our own backyard. And Brandywine Creek State Park is a good place to head. Park near the office and find a trail that leads to the water.

- Suggested Menu -

Aunt Camille's French Onion Soup
(see recipes)

Bob's Toast Points (see recipes)

Crunchy Fresh Vegetables and dip

Patsy's Apple Cake (see recipes)

Fort DuPont

Delaware City, DE 19706

A beautiful spot to catch the crispiness of the air with the beautiful late autumn light on the river with Fort Delaware across the way. This is a barely discovered park that is tucked away off Route 9 right past Delaware City. This was once a vibrant military base that reverberated with military, families and lots of life. We landed here on one of those super still, crisp fall days and just basically lazed the afternoon away gazing out on the river. This is a state park so there is a parking fee.

Bring an elegant picnic here—the tables are quite close to where you can park.

- Suggested Menu -

Brie and Baguette

Roast Pork Tenderloins with Cherries
(see recipes)

Wild Rice Salad (see recipes)

Apple Cobbler (see recipes)

-Winter Picnics -

Yes! Winter Picnics!
And no, I'm not crazy!

Winter picnics have proved to be some of our favorites - mainly because we really enjoy braving the snow and cold. Instead of whining indoors, we set out with our supplies and hot rum toddies and go home warm from the inside out!

The bracing air, the laughs at our craziness for doing such a thing, and the good food we bring with us make a snowstorm something to look forward to! There are a couple of places to go for a winter picnic.

Brandywine Creek State Park
47 Adams Dam Road, Wilmington, DE 19807

Battery Park in Old New Castle
or
your own back yard– the kids will love it!

If you park near the office at Brandywine Creek State Park you will be near the sledders so be sure to bring your sleds along.

Winter and Spring are the seasons that we must catch while we can. Having food in the cupboards, ready to be prepared and packed up for picnicking is a great help so that you can "carpe diem"!

- Suggested Menu -

Tonya's Haystacks (see recipes)

Oranges

Chocolate bars

Brian's Hot Chocolate (see recipes)

or Hot Tea

Hot, Hearty, Easy Soup (See recipes)

Mrs. Hyde's Filled and Frozen Buns (see recipes)

Oranges

Chocolate

Hot dogs are fun to do too!

Just remember to buy a disposable grill at the
end of the summer so that you'll be ready to go!

- Picnics Across the River -

Finding the ideal spot for a sunset picnic in New Castle County is nearly impossible. The sunsets are so beautiful as one drives down I-95 headed south - but oh so elusive! You'll have to go a little further afield. Just a drive across the Delaware Memorial Bridge will take you to a perfect spot to see the sun go down and enjoy the lights of the bridge. We packed out picnic basket on a lovely summer evening and headed over to New Jersey. Looking down as we drove over we could see the boats dotting the water.

Driving Directions:
Go over the Delaware Memorial Bridge– Take the first exit to Pennsville. When you arrive in downtown Pennsville, take a right into the Riverview Park. You won't be secluded there—people strolling and enjoying the summer but check out the sunset!

- Suggested Menu -

Bacon Lettuce & Tomato Sandwiches

Easy to make and easy to transport
BLTs are a must in the summer –
you might even wait to buy some
famous New Jersey tomatoes
at a farm stand in Pennsville.

Beautiful farm stand right there
as you get off the exit.

Cajun Roasted Potatoes

Lemon Chess Tartlets (see recipes)

Hancock House at Hancock's Bridge

Lower Alloway Creek, New Jersey 08038

Being from Old New Castle, we think that we have the corner on the market regarding colonial history. But just over the river and through the woods is a beautiful spot with true history. Southern New Jersey was quite an important place during the Revolutionary War. Stop in the adorable town of Greenwich (pronounced green-witch) at the memorial and then head to Hancock's Bridge. Learn the heroic/tragic story at beautiful Hancock House.

We've been to this lovely spot more than once. Rural, southern New Jersey is worlds away from New Castle County although it is only a 45 minute drive away! We set out to learn some history and ended up having an elegant picnic right on location. Because there is no hiking involved and a picnic table right there, you can plan a very elegant picnic dinner.

- Suggested Menu -

Red Pepper Creamy Soup (see recipes)
Whole Roasted Chicken with Herbs (see recipes)
Herbed Corn on the Cob (see recipes)
Sliced Summer Tomatoes
Raspberries and Cream
Sugar Cookies

- Container Picnics -

Be a Shoebie!
America's answer to the Bento Box!

"Shoebies" are those of us who go on a day trip and bring our lunch in a shoebox. Take your picnic in a shoe box- easy to pack in the car and away you go!

This is a fun way to make use of all your old shoeboxes, delight children with the fun surprises inside their boxes and do away with the cooler and basket.

We love to do this as a variation on a theme. The challenge is for the picnic packer– what treats can you pack away in those shoe boxes?

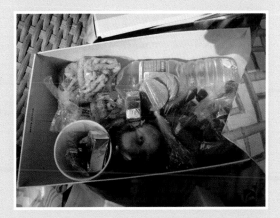

Shoebie Picnic Suggested Snacks

Peanuts in the shell

Little cheeses- Bonbel type

Crackers

Carrot sticks

Individual packages of red licorice or other candies

Sandwich bags of Cheetos or other sturdy chip-type treats

Whole apple

Cookies

Little boxes of juices, Water

Italian cheeses and meats rolled up with swab of mayonnaise and a leaf of basil

Thin slices of smoked deli turkey with a swab of mayonnaise,
a thin slice of red pepper and baby spinach

Buttered rolls

Cocktail size clear plastic cups with pasta salad

Devilled egg shooters-one devilled egg
placed wide end down in individual Dixie cups

- Bento Boxes -

Instead of a big submarine sandwich from the deli (even though they can hit the spot at certain times), do a delicate picnic the Japanese way. This is a perfect, elegant idea for a cocktail picnic. Such possibilities!

Suggestons for your Bento Boxes

Sushi

Cucumbers and other crunchy vegetables with

Tzatziki Sauce for dipping (see recipes)

Hard Boiled Eggs

Heirloom Cherry Tomatoes with

gin and sea salt for dipping

Paté and Cornichons with fancy crackers

Sliced Chicken with pesto sauce

Fresh Fruit-cherries or grapes or one big fruit /halved

Shrimp Catalan (see recipes)

Pasta Salad

- Recipes -

Cold Avocado and Cucumber Soup

2 unpeeled English cucumbers, coarsely chopped

2 ripe avocados, peeled, pitted
and flesh scooped out

1 tablespoon Vidalia or other sweet onion, chopped

2/3 cup plain Greek yogurt

1/3 cup whole milk

1 small can vegetable broth

1 tablespoon lemon juice

1 teaspoon mild vinegar

1 tablespoon mint, chopped

Pinch ground cayenne

Pinch salt

Place all ingredients in blender and
puree 3-4 minutes until smooth.

Add a little water if the soup is too thick.

Cover and refrigerate for 4 hours or overnight.

Quinoa Salad

Quinoa salad can really be a staple of any picnic. There are so many ways to prepare it – you can use almost any ingredients and dressing and you won't go wrong.

Start with cooked quinoa.
(Follow directions on the package.)

Make a Tabbouleh using cherry tomatoes, parsley, scallions and mint leaves, chopped.

Make a light dressing with
1 tablespoon of lemon juice and
4 tablespoons of extra–virgin olive oil,
1/2 teaspoon of salt, a hearty shake
of coarsely ground pepper
and 1/4 teaspoon of dried mustard.

or

Combine chopped macadamia nuts,
a clove of garlic, a chopped scallion, a seeded,
diced cucumber, a diced green apple,
some diced celery and a seeded
and chopped jalapeno pepper.

Make a dressing of non fat plain Greek yogurt,
lemon juice and a little salt.

or

Throw some of your left over vegetables together
with some crunchy ones with your favorite dressing.

Cold Curry of Zucchini Soup

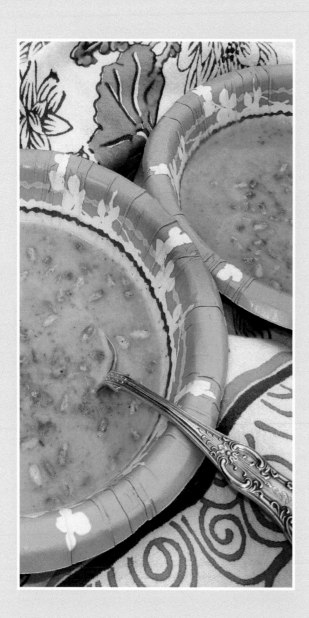

3 tablespoons butter, more as needed

1 onion chopped

2 cloves garlic, minced or pressed

1/2 teaspoon ground cumin

1/2 teaspoon ground coriander

1/2 teaspoon ground ginger

2 teaspoons curry powder-more or less
depending on what you like

2 lbs. zucchini peeled and diced

4 cups vegetable or chicken broth – more
if you'd like the soup thinner

Salt

1 cup half and half or milk

Grated orange peel and sunflower seeds for garnish.

Melt butter in large pot and
sauté onion and garlic with spices.

Add zucchini and more
butter if necessary and continue to cook through.

Add vegetable broth.

Cover and simmer for about a half an hour.

Add salt to taste. Puree soup in blender.

Stir in milk or half and half.

Refrigerate until you're ready to leave for the picnic.

Ann's Blueberry Muffins

Use cupcake liners in your muffin tins for these.

2 cups Bisquick

1/2 teaspoon cinnamon

1 cup sour cream

1/4 cup sugar

1 egg

1 cup berries

Mix dry ingredients. Add sour cream and egg.

Stir with a fork. (never over stir muffins).

Add blueberries.

Sprinkle each muffin with 1/2 teaspoon sugar.

Bake in a 425° oven for about 20 minutes.

Hearty Sandwiches

Not that you need to know how to make a sandwich but here are some ideas and tips to make your sandwiches for your picnics a little more interesting. Pack all your ingredients separately and assemble the sandwich on the spot. This keeps things from getting soggy and squished together. Mayonnaise can be brought in a small container and carried next to your cold drink and the most study items can be packed near the bottom in ascending order with the bread on top. It's not a bad idea to throw in a pickle or two and fancy relishes etc.

Fun combos:

Always start with good bread!
Cheddar, tomatoes and arugula,
mayonnaise, salt and pepper

—

Cheddar, cucumber and marmalade on
pumpernickel bread

—

Sliced turkey and thinly sliced apple
on whole wheat bread
with maple mayonnaise
(combine 1/4 cup mayo with
1 and 1/2 teaspoons maple syrup)

—

Instead of egg salad, slice hard boiled eggs
and spread bread with basil butter.
Basil butter– combine 6 tablespoons of unsalted butter,
3/4 teaspoon lemon juice, 3 tablespoons finely chopped
basil and 1 small clove of garlic, minced.

—

Shrimp Salad –buy unseasoned cooked shrimp,
chop it and add mayo, a little tarragon,
chopped chives and lemon juice– all to taste.

—

Tenderloin or marinated flank steak sandwiches
with Dijon mustard and Gorgonzola
(Cooked beef is always best served at room temperature
without ever having been refrigerated.)

—

Grilled Portobello Mushrooms

Roasted Tomatoe Soup

This soup is absolute heaven in the deepest days of summer when the tomatoes are bursting with color and flavor!

5 lbs. summer tomatoes, cut in half

3 red or sweet onions, cut into wedges

A clove or two of garlic

Extra virgin olive oil

Celery salt

1 and 1/2 teaspoon sugar

Place tomatoes and onions in a single layer,
drizzle with 5 tablespoons olive oil and
roast in a 450° degree oven for 20 minutes.

When cool enough to handle put them in
a blender with onions, roasting juices.

5 tablespoons of oil, salt dash of celery salt,
black pepper and sugar.

Blend and strain though a strainer.
It takes a while to work the
tomato mixture through the strainer.

Put the strainer over a deep pot or bowl and keep
mashing it around from time to time.
You'll have a lot of left over mixture
(mostly seeds and tomato skins).

Chill until ready to picnic.

Blueberry Tarts

Refrigerated Pie Crust

Cupcake liners

4 cups Blueberries

2 tablespoons cornstarch mixed
with 1/4 cup water
and 3/4—1 cup sugar
(depending on the sweetness of the berries)
and 1/2 teaspoon cinnamon

Place foil cup cake liners in the muffin tins.

Roll out the pie crust using
a little flour to make it thinner.

Cut the crust with a cookie cutter or the rim of
glass to the size of the liners.

Mix the berries and the sugar/cornstarch
mixture in muffin tins.

Dot with butter.

Decorate with a criss cross of pie crust.

Bake at 450° for 10 minutes and then
reduce heat to 350° and bake for 1/2 hour
or so until fruit is bubbling and
crust is lightly browned.

Lemon Chess Tartlets

These are easy and delicious!

Roll out pie crust with a little flour to make it thinner.

Using a cookie cutter or the rim of a glass cut pie crust out to the size of foil cupcake liners and then wedge them in the muffin tins. Leave them in the cupcake liners when transporting to the picnic.
(Leave the muffin tins at home.)

2 cups sugar

1 tablespoons flour

1 tablespoons cornmeal

4 eggs

1/4 cup butter melted

1/4 cup milk

2 tablespoons grated lemon rind

1/4 cup lemon juice

Pie crust for 1 pie
(I use refrigerated packaged pie crust)

Combine, sugar, flour and cornmeal.

Add remaining ingredients; beat until smooth.

Spoon into the lined muffin tins.

Bake in a 350° oven for about 25-30 minutes until golden brown and almost set.

Red Pepper Creamy Soup

2 lbs. red bell peppers,
seeded and cut into quarters
1 small Vidalia onion, minced

1 large baking potato, peeled and diced

1 and 1/3 cups vegetable broth

1 and 1/2 teaspoons sea salt

1/3 cup heavy cream

Steam peppers until very soft,
about 45 minutes.

Let cool and then slip skins off.

Simmer (covered) the onion, potato and
broth abut 25 minutes until very soft.

Combine all ingredients in a food processor or
blender—blend and chill until picnic time.

Whole Roast Chicken with Herbs

What's great about this is that you take it
right from the oven, in the roasting
pan (carefully placed in the car!)

Line your pan with extra long pieces of foil
so that you can wrap up the bird after cooking.

Follow your easiest recipe for roast chicken.

I like to put halved lemons and limes in the cavity
or fill with onions, celery and herbs.
It looks pretty to sprinkle
fresh herbs over the breasts and legs –
sage and rosemary are wonderful.

Drizzle over top some lemon juice and olive oil.

If there is a lot of fat in the roasting pan,
spoon it out at home
(this avoids messes in the car!)

Aunt Camille's French Onion Soup with Bob's Toast Points

My husband's great Aunt Camille was actually French so you know this is good. Make your toasts with melted cheese before you leave for your picnic.

From her cookbook:

"Slice very thinly 5 large onions,
heat 1/3 cup butter in heavy saucepan,
add the onion rings, cook them over low flame,
stirring constantly until rings are
an even golden brown.

Sprinkle with 1 tablespoon of flour
and when well blended gradually pour in
6 cups beef consommé, stirring constantly until
the soup begins to boil. Add 1 tablespoon sugar.

Lower the heat, cover the pan,
simmer very gently for 15-20 minutes.

Substitute vegetable or mushroom broth
for the consommé for a vegetarian option.

Bob's Toast Points

Pre heat oven to 250°.

Line a large baking sheet with silver paper.

Cover with olive oil.
Slice baguette or
other good bread into thin slices.
Flip bread over so
that it is thoroughly covered.

Sprinkle with pepper,
dried Herbes de Provence .

Bake for about 1/2 hour.

Rub cheese on toasties (if desired)
and under the broiler for about 1 minute or so
until the cheese is melted and
the edges are brown.

Watch carefully!

Roasted Cherry Tomatoes

4 cups summer cherry tomatoes, various colors

4 garlic cloves, skin left on and crushed

5 sprigs of fresh thyme

Sea salt, pepper and sugar

Extra virgin olive oil

Parchment paper

Cut tomatoes in half and
place on the parchment paper
on a baking sheet, skin side up.

Place the garlic in various spots on the pan and pull
off some of the thyme leaves and sprinkle around.

Season with salt and pepper
and a sprinkling of sugar.

Drizzle 3 tablespoons or so of olive oil over all.

Bake in preheated 275° oven
for 1 and 3/4 hours - 2 and 1/2 hours.

Patsy's Apple Cake

5 apples, 6 tablespoons sugar,

2 teaspoons cinnamon,

4 eggs, 2 and 1/3 cups sugar,

1 cup vegetable oil,

1/3 cup orange juice, 2 teaspoons vanilla,

3 cups flour, 1 and 1/2 teaspoons baking soda,

1 and 1/2 teaspoons baking powder,

1/2 teaspoon salt

Peel and pare apples and slice thin.

Combine sugar and cinnamon
and mix into the apples.

With an electric mixer, blend eggs, sugar, oil,
orange juice and vanilla. In separate bowl,
combine flour, baking soda and salt.

Add to liquid ingredients and blend with mixer.

Continue mixing until thick and lemon colored.

Grease and flour a Bundt pan.

Layer the batter and then the apples,
beginning and ending with the batter.

Bake in a 350° oven for about 1 and 1/2 hours.

Cool on rack for 10 minutes and
then invert onto a platter.

Antipasto

Somehow this works on a picnic.

I like to serve it chopped with the meats, cheeses and lettuce, served with the condiments on the side.

Combine the salad at home and carry the dressing and condiments separately.

Arrange on a platter and toss with the dressing.

Buy in whatever quantity you need:

Ham   Provolone cheese   Pepperoni

Capicola   Genoa Salami   Prosciutto

Any other Italian meats and cheeses you like

Marinated artichoke hearts

Jumbo pitted black olives

Marinated button mushrooms

Canned anchovies

Hot peppers

Cold Zucchini Soup

4 small zucchini

1/2 green pepper, chopped

1 sweet onion, chopped

10.5 oz can vegetable broth

3 sprigs parsley

1/4 teaspoon dried dill

Salt and pepper

1 scant cup of Greek yogurt

1 jalapeno, seeded

Cook zucchini, green pepper, onion and broth for 20 minutes. Put in blender and add parsley, dill, salt and pepper, sour cream and jalapeno.

Blend until creamy and smooth.
Chill or if it's a cool day heat and put in pre warmed thermos when ready to leave.

Bob's Pierogi

Thaw a package of Mrs. T's pierogi.

Brown lightly in butter in a frying pan.

Top with shredded Parmigiano/
Reggiano cheese.

For a BLT pierogi (minus the lettuce) top with
a tiny bit of cooked bacon
and a half of cherry tomato.

Salade Niçoise

Easy to prepare and pack.
Pack everything separately and
assemble on the spot.
It's better, really, if everything is room temperature
so you don't need to fret too much
about it being in the cooler.

Be sure to include tuna
(high quality canned is fine),
tomatoes, cucumber, green beans,
pitted black olives, quartered red potatoes,
hard boiled eggs, anchovies and lettuce.

Serve with a mild French dressing.

Watermelon Barley / Black Eyed Pea Salad

My husband, who doesn't like watermelon nor barley, loved this!

1 and 1/2 cups barley, salt,

1/4 diced red onion, 1/2 cup olive oil,

1 green pepper, diced

1/4 cup red wine vinegar,

2 cups diced watermelon

1 cup canned black eyed peas

1 cup halved heirloom cherry tomatoes

1 English cucumber, peeled, seeded and diced

1 garlic clove minced

1 cup crumbled feta cheese

1/2 cup chopped parsley

1/4 cup chopped dill

Cook barley in 2 quarts of salted water.

Bring water to a boil, reduce heat and simmer for about 30 minutes until al dente.

Drain and cool

Combine red onion, olive oil, green pepper, vinegar, and garlic. Add to the barley.

Add the rest of the ingredients and toss.

Serve at room temperature or chilled.

Blodg's Blueberry Dessert

Good to assemble ahead as the tastes meld together

Fresh blueberries

Sour cream

Brown sugar

Layer the ingredients in plastic cups .

End with a sprinkle of brown sugar.

Don't forget spoons!

Roasted Cajun Potatoes

1 and 1/2 ear of corn per person/
each ear of corn halved

Grill cooked corn on charcoal or
gas grill or under the broiler.
Keep an eye on it and remember to turn it.

After grilling, toss it in a bowl
with 1/4 cup fresh cilantro or
2 tablespoons chopped fresh basil to
1 tablespoon fresh lime juice and
1 tablespoon oil oil.

Amounts vary according to
how many ears of corn you have.

Shute House Tomato Tart

We were on a trip touring gardens in Dorset, England

and begged this recipe from the cook, Jane, of Shute
House where we had lunch.

For the crust:

Buy a refrigerated crust and gently press
the poppy seeds in the dough but don't overwork it.

or

2 cups of flour, 1 stick of butter, 3 tablespoons water,

3 oz poppy seeds, black pepper, 1 egg,

Couple of teaspoons of water,

1 tablespoon brown sugar

Combine all ingredients (don't overwork the dough)
and press into a disposable pie tin.

Bake the crust "blind"-line the aluminum,
disposable pie tin and prick the crust all over.

Bake in a preheated 450° oven for 12-15 minutes.

For the filling

8 red onions, sliced   4 cans (14 oz) chopped tomatoes

1 small can tomato paste   1 tablespoon brown sugar

Grated good quality cheddar cheese

Sliced black olives

Fry the onions in large skillet, slowly, for 30-45 minutes.

Mixed chopped tomatoes, tomato paste
and brown sugar and place on top of onions.

Simmer slowly for 30-45 minutes.

Let mixture cool a bit and place in baked pie crust.

Sprinkle with cheddar cheese and
decorate with black olives.

Bake in 350° oven until cheese melts
and has just started to turn brown.

Cool and serve at room temperature.

Wild Rice Salad

1 cup uncooked wild rice or wild rice mix

1 cup chopped pecans

1 cup dried cranberries

4 sliced green onions and tops

1/4 cup olive oil

1/3 cup orange juice

1/8 teaspoon salt

1-2 tablespoons Balsamic Vinegar

Combine 3 cups of vegetable broth
and rice in a saucepan.

Cook according to direction
until rice has just opened.

Drain and place in a bowl.

Add remaining ingredients and mix well.

Roast Pork with Cherries

Two 1 lb. pork tenderloins

1/2 cup dried cherries

1/2 cup dry red wine

1/4 cup balsamic vinegar

3/4 cup real cranberry juice

4 cloves of garlic, minced

1 large onion, chopped

2 teaspoons dried rosemary

2 tablespoons olive oil

Salt and pepper to taste.

Place all ingredients except pork
in a bowl and whisk together.
Then put in plastic bag that will fit
the pork tenderloins, too. Shake vigorously.

Heat olive oil in frying pan and
brown the tenderloins on all side.

Place in roasting pan and pour marinade all over it.
Roast in a 375° oven about 20-25 minutes.

Test with a meat thermometer which
should read 150-155° degrees.

Take out of oven, put pork on
a platter and let cool.

Wrap the platter so the juice
won't spill and carve it at the picnic.

Apple Cobbler

This is delicious warm or cold.

Add a few dollops of whipped cream.
In the bottom of a 9 x 11 baking dish,
place 5-6 cups thinly sliced apples that have
been mixed with 1/2 to 3/4 cups of sugar,
1/4 teaspoon cinnamon and 1/8 teaspoon nutmeg.

Double this amount of fruit, sugar and
spices if it looks skimpy.

2 cups of bisquick, 2 sticks of butter,

2 cups of sugar and 2 cups of milk.

Melt the butter and
add the other ingredients.

Pour over the fruit.

Bake in a 350° oven for 45-60 minutes.

Portable Pots-de-Crème

Make these in individual, plastic Dixie cups.

1 package chocolate bits,

4 tablespoons cold water

5 eggs, separated

Whipped cream

Separate eggs and beat the whites
until stiff and the yolks until well beaten.

Combine chocolate bits and the water and
stir over low heat until well blended.

Remove from heat and slowly stir in egg yolks.
Fold in the egg whites and
mix gently until well blended.

Spoon into plastic cups and
refrigerate over night.

Serve with a dollop of whipped cream
(or Reddi-whip) at the picnic.

Tonya's Haystacks

Your favorite chili recipe

Fritos (regular kind)

grated cheddar cheese

Sour cream

Put Fritos in bottom of paper bowl,
cover with a hearty portion of chili,
followed by the cheddar cheese
and topped with the sour cream.

Brian's Hot Chocolate

25.6 oz. non fat dry milk

1 and 1/2 cup non dairy creamer (6 oz. jar)

3 cups instant cocoa mix– 16 oz. package

1 and 1/2 cup confectioner's sugar

1 and 1/2 cup mini marshmallows

Mix in large bowl and store in airtight container.

Take what you think you'll need on your picnic.

Fill mug 1/2 full of mix and top with hot water.
(Preheat your thermos before
filling with boiling hot water.
Or do ahead and fill your thermos
with the hot chocolate.)

Hot, Hardy Easy Soup

1 large can of tomato soup

1 can beef bouillon

2 cans pea soup

Curry powder to taste

Sherry to taste
Mix the soups together, and half the
amount of water called for and heat.
Add the curry and sherry .
(It is for a winter picnic so be generous with the sherry!)

Top each cup with a dollop of sour cream.

Mrs. Hyde's
Filled and Frozen Buns

Hearty Rolls like Ciabatta or
other crusty rolls, buttered

Finely cubed ham, finely cubed cheddar cheese,
minced onion and mayonnaise

or

Cooked bacon chopped fine,
spicy jalapeño cheese,
minced onion and mayonnaise

Mix the ingredients for the sandwiches together
and spread on the buttered rolls.

Wrap in foil and freeze.

Before leaving on your picnic heat wrapped
buns in 400° oven and bake for 1/2 hour.

Tzatziki Sauce

1/2 cup plain Greek yogurt

1/3 cup sour cream

1/2 cup peeled, grated cucumber,
squeezed dry

1 teaspoon minced garlic

1 tablespoon extra virgin olive oil

1 tablespoon chopped mint leaves or fresh dill

juice of 1/2 lemon

1 teaspoon lemon zest

Salt to taste

Freshly ground pepper to taste.

Combine the yogurt, sour cream,
cucumbers and garlic in a food processor
and puree until smooth. Transfer to a bowl
and fold in the olive oil, mint or dill,
lemon juice and lemon zest.

Season with salt and pepper.

Chill until picnic time.

Shrimp Catalan

1 lb. large shrimp, 1/3 cup olive oil, 2 tablespoons,
chopped toasted almonds

1 teaspoon minced garlic, 1 teaspoon paprika,

1 tablespoon chopped parsley,

1/2 plum tomato, seeded and diced,

1 teaspoon sea salt

Add 2 tablespoons of the olive oil to the pan.
When the oil is just beginning to smoke,
add the shrimp.

Sauté on medium high until done – about 2-3 minutes.

Toss with remaining ingredients.

Serve at room temperature.

Cucumber Dill Soup

3 medium cucumbers, peeled, seeded
and cut into chunks

1 and 1/2 cups vegetable broth

1 cup sour cream

1/2 cup buttermilk

1/2 cup yogurt

2 and 1/2 tablespoons white wine vinegar

1 garlic clove, minced

2 green onions sliced thin

Salt to taste

2 tablespoons dill, chopped

Process the cucumber in a food
processor with 1/2 cup of
broth. Do not over blend.

In a large bowl, combine all remaining
ingredients, including the cucumbers.
Mix well and chill until picnic time.

Texas Fudge

6 cups Cheddar cheese, shredded

2 cups Monterey Jack cheese, shredded or cubed

12 oz. jar jalapeno peppers, sliced

6 - 7 large eggs

Paprika

Spray bottom of large oblong baking dish
with cooking spray.

Fill bottom of pan with 4 cups
of the Cheddar cheese.

Place the peppers evenly over the cheese.

Add the Monterey Jack cheese over that.

Scramble the eggs and
pour over the cheese and peppers.

Cover with the remaining cheddar cheese.

Sprinkle with paprika.

Bake in a 375° oven for 40-45 minutes.

Cook and cut into one inch squares.

Chicken and Veggie Skewers

Chicken breasts, mushroom caps,
broccoli florets, slices of small zucchini,
chunks of sweet onions or any vegetable that you like.

Cube chicken breasts into bite size pieces and let
marinate in your favorite marinade.

Cook in frying pan and let cool separately.

Do the same with the vegetables.

Cook each one separately and let cool.

Don't overcook! Before leaving for your
picnic thread each item onto skewers.

Make sure the chicken is fully cooked– that way,
if a disaster befalls and you can't use the grill

– they'll still be delicious!

Liza's Fruit Smoothies

1 peach non-fat yogurt

1 banana

4 ice cubes

1 and 1/2 cups frozen pineapple chunks

6 oz. Ensure vanilla protein drink

Whir all ingredients together in a blender.
Top with any seasonal fruit.

Curry of Eggplant Soup

3 tablespoons butter, more as needed

1 onion chopped

2 cloves garlic, minced or pressed

1/2 teaspoon ground cumin

1/2 teaspoon ground coriander

1/2 teaspoon ground ginger

2 teaspoons curry powder -

more or less depending on what you like

2 lbs. eggplant, peeled and diced

4 cups vegetable broth

Salt

1 cup half and half or milk

Melt butter and sauté onion
and garlic with spices.
Add eggplant and more butter if needed
and continue to cook through.
Simmer, covered and cook for 45 minutes to an hour.
Ad salt to taste.
Puree in blender, stir in half and half.

Refrigerate until you're ready
to leave for the picnic.

Cold Cream of Curry Soup

3 cups plain, non fat Greek yogurt

3 cups vegetable broth

1 clove garlic, chopped

1 and 1/2 teaspoons curry powder

Chives or tops of scallions, for garnish

Put all ingredients in the blender and blend.
Serve cold, topped with chopped chives

Presto! Perfect picnic soup!

- Picnics and our mental health -

Picnics are good for the soul. We live in a world of hustle and bustle. So many people are anxious and depressed with their situations. Family problems, financial problems, tension at work can tend to be overwhelming. The stress of our everyday lives can leave us depleted and without joy. In the winter we are holed up in our houses and in the summer we go from refrigerated box to refrigerated box and sometimes forget to take advantage of all that nature has to offer us. Picnics can be an avenue for getting centered, reducing the stress in our lives and renewing relationships.

Being in tune with nature is being in tune with our rhythms and the universe. Lying on a picnic blanket staring at the sky or seeing the sun glimmer on the water is a way to renew ourselves. Being in a scene that is not home and work revitalizes us.

Families, too, can benefit from the togetherness of an outdoors picnic. Families today are on the go with activities, sports events, camps and so on. So often family time is spent together in front of the television or on the run. Being together in an unstructured environment, talking and relaxing creates new energy and dynamics within the family. Children can learn new skills in helping organize the picnic food and gear which will improve their developmental skills.

A few years ago, not wanting to waste a precious summer evening, we dedicated Tuesday as Picnic Night. It has become a permanent rite of our summers as much as tennis games, softball leagues, walks around the track or whatever activity you do on a summer's evening. Someone asked me, "What do you do on a picnic?" Actually, you don't "do" anything. Picnics are not about activity. Picnics are about relaxing and communing with nature and your companions.

Ask yourself this:
When was the last time you just sat and gazed at the trees and the birds and the bugs and felt the silence and wonder of the universe?
Sometimes doing something different requires a little bit of planning and effort. If you make just the teensiest effort with a picnic you never know what worlds may open up to you.

- In Conclusion -

As you can see, we've had the time of our lives exploring and finding perfect picnic spots and the meals to go with them. It is my sincere hope that you have the same experience. As you pack your basket with good food and set out on your picnics, I wish you the best of times enjoying all that you experience together in this old fashioned way.

Happy Picnicking!